MYSTERIOUS ENCOUNTERS

23.70/18.86 ea. All 8 for 189.60/150.88

Accelerated Reader Disk:

Is it a pirates ghost or a mind playing tricks? Eyewitness accounts paired with alternative explanations make this a favorite for readers.

KIDHAVEN, Grades 4-8, 2006-2007, 48 Pages, 6" x 9", color photos and illustrations, Table of Contents, Index, and Glossary

SOCIAL SCIENCES & CONTEMPORARY ISSUES

ANGELS - Lynett, Rachel

BIGFOOT - Woog, Adam

DRAGONS - Brucken, Kelli M

GHOSTS - Brucken, Kelli M

HAUNTED HOUSES - Brucken, Kelli M

LOCH NESS MONSTER, THE - Parks, Peggy J

VAMPIRES - McMeans, Bonnie

WEREWOLVES - Hirschmann, Kris

Mysterious Encounters

Ghosts

by Kelli M. Brucken

KIDHAVEN PRESS

An imprint of Thomson Gale, a part of The Thomson Corporation

THOMSON

GALE

0 0022 0306562 4

Detroit • New York • San Francisco • San Diego • New Haven, Conn • Waterville, Maine • London • Munich

For more information, contact
KidHaven Press
27500 Drake Rd.
Farmington Hills, MI 48331-3535
Or you can visit our Internet site at http://www.gale.com

LIBRARY OF CONGRESS CATALOGING-IN-PUBLICATION DATA

Brucken, Kelli M., 1974-
  Ghosts / by Kelli M. Brucken.
    p. cm. — (Encounters with)
  Includes bibliographical references and index.
  ISBN 0-7377-3474-4 (hardcover : alk. paper) 1. Ghosts—Juvenile literature.
  I. Title. II. Series.
  BF1461.B82 2006
  133.1—dc22
                                                                    2005021200

Printed in the United States of America

Contents

Chapter 1

The World of Ghosts

Rattling chains, heavy footsteps, slamming doors, and moaning cries. Those are sounds many people associate with ghosts. Are these signs of real ghosts?

Some people think that ghosts are simply imagined. They believe that all strange occurrences can be explained by science. Other people believe in a **supernatural** world. Many of these people are believers because they have had a personal experience with what they say is a ghost.

What Are Ghosts?

Science has not proven that ghosts exist or that they do not exist. This has led to many theories to explain the thousands and thousands of ghostly experiences people have reported throughout the world.

Most people think that ghosts are spirits of dead people that are somehow stuck on Earth. Long-time ghost hunter Hans Holzer says, "A ghost is a human being who has passed out of the physical body."[1] Holzer believes ghosts become trapped in the physical world. Usually this is due to some kind of trauma, such as a violent or untimely death.

The History of Ghosts

The mystery of ghost sightings goes back many centuries, and ghost stories are a part of every culture on Earth. Some of the earliest ghost stories were written in **hieroglyphics** by the ancient Egyptians around 4000 B.C.

Many people believe that the spirit leaves the body when a person dies. Ghosts might be spirits that become trapped in our physical world.

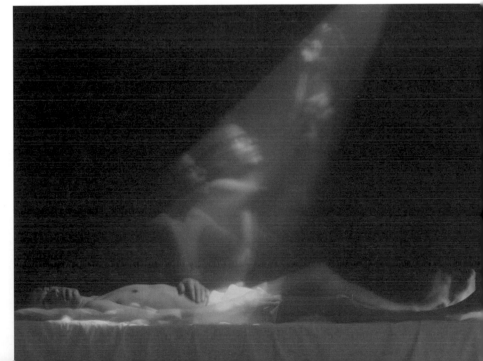

The Ghost Hunter

Hanz Holzer is an expert on ghosts. He has investigated ghost sightings all over the world. Although Holzer believes he has found much evidence of ghosts, he has never proven that they exist.

The Ba and the Ka

The Egyptians believed the human soul was composed of many parts. Two of these parts were called the ba and the ka. The Egyptians imagined the ba and ka to be ghostlike figures that stayed close to a dead body to protect it.

The ba was portrayed as a bird with a human head. The ka was like a person's invisible twin. After death the ka stayed with the dead body while the ba roamed the night.

It was thought the ka must be appeased by humans. Priests of the time would make daily offerings of food and drink. If a priest did not please a ka, it was said the ka would leave its place by the body and haunt the living.

Ghosts were also a part of the culture of ancient Greece, but they did not cause any harm. **Grecian** ghosts were said to reside in the underworld called Hades. It was said that when a person died, his or her spirit would rise from the body with screams as it journeyed to Hades.

Once in the underworld, the ghosts were said to stand around whispering to each other, complaining about the loss of the pleasures they enjoyed while they were living. Sometimes the Greek people would have special ceremonies to call the spirits to the world of the living, to talk with them, or ask for advice. When the ghosts made their appearance, they were described as little puffs of smoke with little or no power to harm the living.

Appearing as a bird with a human head, the ba of a dead Egyptian pharaoh hovers over his lifeless body.

The ancient Romans also encountered ghosts. The Roman **historian** known as Pliny the Younger authored one of the earliest written ghost stories in A.D. 1000.

Arthenodorus and the Ghost

Pliny wrote of a pleasant and large house in Athens that contained a ghost. In the dead of night, the sound of clanking metal followed by the clatter of chains and the appearance of a ghost could be heard in the house.

The ghost was described as "a gaunt, ragged old man, with a long beard and shaggy hair. [His] feet were fettered [chained] and with his hands he shook the **manacles** that bound his wrists."[2]

The owners of the house were scared by the ghost, so they abandoned it. They put up a sign offering the house for rent or sale, hoping that someone who had not heard of the ghost would want it.

The **philosopher** Arthenodorus happened upon the house and was interested in the very low price. He asked around, found out the facts, and in spite of (or perhaps because of) the ghost, decided to rent the house.

One night, while Arthenodorus was working, the ghost paid him a visit. The figure stood rattling his chains and moaning, motioning that Arthenodorus should follow it. Not at all frightened by such an appearance, he followed the ghost out into the courtyard, where the spirit abruptly vanished.

A ghost in chains motions the Greek philosopher
Arthenodorus outside to his burial spot.

Arthenodorus had a plan. He marked with leaves the exact spot in the yard where the ghost had disappeared. The next morning he called officials to come and dig up the spot. Low and behold, a human skeleton wrapped in chains was found under the ground.

The bones were gathered and given a proper burial. This must have been what the ghost was seeking, as it was never seen in the house again. The practice of helping a ghost move on to the other side is followed all over of the world.

Ghostly Rituals

Many cultures have rituals to help the spirits of the dead move on to the next world. Even today, in some Asian countries such as India, Bangladesh, Sri

Wearing elaborate wooden masks, young Dogon men in Mali perform a funeral dance to help the dead pass into the spirit world.

Lanka, China, and Afghanistan, the thumbs and big toes of a dead person are tied together with pieces of white cotton cloth. This is done to keep the person's spirit from escaping the body as well as to keep evil spirits from entering and taking over the body after death.

The Dogon people of West Africa still practice traditional death rituals. They believe spirits of the dead hate to leave behind their homes and villages. It is said the spirits often return to cause trouble, disrupt households, and even bring droughts and disease.

Young men of the Dogon tribes perform a funeral dance to help the spirit move on to the next world. Each dancer wears a mask that shows some part of life the spirit may miss, such as an animal or person. When the ghost sees these symbols it is thought they have a chance to say goodbye and travel peacefully into the spirit world.

Some cultures believe if they confuse the spirits, the ghosts will be too busy to haunt anyone. Ancient customs of some aborigine tribes in Australia called for the people to cut off the head of their dead. The thought was that the spirit would be too

Ghostly Appearances

A national poll found that 51 percent of Americans believe in ghosts. Most of these people said they have *seen* a ghost, one-half have *heard* a ghost, one-fourth have *felt* a ghost, and one-fifth have *spoken* with a ghost.

busy looking for its head to worry about haunting the living.

In nineteenth-century Europe and America, the dead were carried out of the house feet first. This was to stop the spirit from looking back into the house and calling other members of the family to follow it.

Another early American custom was to cover mirrors in black fabric. This was so the soul would not get trapped in the mirror, keeping it from traveling to the spirit world.

Today's Customs

Some early customs of Europe and America are still in practice today, such as wearing black to a funeral. Originally, people wore black to make themselves invisible to the spirits. Today's custom of allowing the cars in a funeral procession to stay together comes from the belief that any delay caused when transporting a soul may turn it into a restless ghost.

Throughout the ages and around the world peole have described all different sorts of encounters with ghosts. Not all encounters are the same, however. Some ghosts are described as friendly or helpful, some are indifferent, and some can be downright nasty.

Chapter 2

Messenger Ghosts

One of the most common types of ghosts encountered is a messenger ghost. A messenger ghost is usually said to be seen by the living family members of a recently deceased person. It seems these ghosts return to tell their families they are happy and not to grieve for them.

Grandfather's Ghost

Gladys Watson of Indianapolis, Indiana, had such an encounter with the ghost of her grandfather. In June 1923 Gladys was getting ready to have a baby. She was excited about her family meeting the new arrival. She had plans to visit her parents and her grandfather in Wilmington, Delaware.

A common type of ghost people report seeing is a messenger ghost, the spirit of a loved one that returns with news from beyond the grave.

One night Gladys woke up from a sound sleep, thinking she had heard someone call her name. As she sat up and looked around, she saw her grandfather standing at the foot of her bed.

Before Gladys could say anything, her grandfather spoke. He told her not to be scared, that it was only him. He went on to say that he had just died. As tears began to fall on Gladys's cheeks, her grandfather pointed to his black suit and bow tie and told her that was what he was going to be buried in. "I just wanted to tell you that I've been waiting to go ever since Ad was taken."[3] (Ad, Gladys's grandmother, had died several years before.)

After her grandfather vanished, Gladys woke her husband to tell him of the visit. Her husband was convinced the incident was a dream, reassuring Gladys that though he was old, her grandfather was very healthy.

But Gladys could not be consoled. She was sure she had seen her grandfather and that he was dead. Although it was only 4:05 in the morning, Gladys's husband phoned her parents.

Gladys's mother answered the phone and was quite surprised by the call. She had not been asleep though, because the grandfather, who had suddenly taken sick during the day, had just died. It turned out that the grandfather had died less than 30 minutes before he appeared at the foot of Gladys's bed.

The appearance of Gladys's grandfather, though disturbing, could be described as a comforting visit. His spirit seemed to want to sooth Gladys, letting her know he was happy and finally with his beloved wife.

Dreaming of Ghosts

Many ghost sightings occur just before a person falls asleep or wakes up. Experts believe the brain sometimes gets confused when it switches between wakefulness and sleep. This confusion can cause visions such as seeing ghosts.

What Lies Beyond?

Sometimes ghosts return to fulfill a promise they made to a living relative. In the book *Ghosts, Spirits, and Hauntings* by Patricia Telesco, Fay Esan tells of a ghostly encounter with her recently deceased mother. This is her story in her own words:

> My mother suffered congestive heart failure when she was 61, and had a heart attack six months later. Upon returning home from the hospital, we began to speculate about what lies ahead when we die. She laughed, saying that, if she passed on before I did, she would let me know that there was an afterlife—by knocking three times. This signal would tell me she was with me, and all was well. Of course I agreed to do the same, should I go first.
>
> In September of 1975, mom called me downstairs wanting to talk about a vision she had the night before. She was in a long dark corridor, with people before and behind her. Ahead was a door that, when opened, revealed the most beautiful garden imaginable, filled with flowers, trees, brooks, and happy people. As she attempted to cross the threshold of the doorway, a figure stopped her and said it was not yet time, but would be soon. The figure gently pulled her out of line and sent her back. At this point mom found herself in bed, taking the vi-

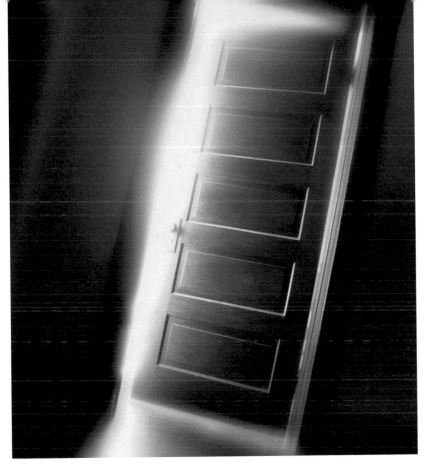

Some people think of entering the afterlife as walking through a door to a beautiful new world.

sion as a portent of her death. Not long thereafter she had another heart attack and was pronounced dead at the hospital.

Six months later, I was suddenly wakened from my sleep. When I looked around, a shadowy figure appeared at my bedside. As soon as my eyes focused on the figure, I heard three resounding raps on the nightstand. That was mom's signal, letting me know that consciousness did, indeed, go on after death. Her promise was fulfilled.[4]

The Will

Another reason for the appearance of a messenger ghost may be to right a wrong. This was the situation when the ghost of James Chaffin visited his son, also named James.

In the early 1900s James Chaffin Sr. was a farmer in North Carolina. He had four sons: Marshall, John, James, and Abner. For some reason, when James Sr. made out his will he left his farm and all his possessions to Marshall. He left nothing to his wife and other three boys.

Some time later James Sr. changed his mind about the will. After reading a particular passage in the *Bible* he decided to change his will. He split everything evenly between his four boys and told them to take care of their mother.

James Sr. hid this new will in his father's old *Bible*. He placed it on the page which held the special passage. Why the will was hidden, and why James Sr. did not mention it to anyone, is unknown.

He did leave a note, however, that told the reader to look at the 27th chapter of Genesis in the *Bible*. He put the note in an inside pocket of his overcoat and stitched the pocket closed.

In 1921 James Chaffin Sr. died. The old will was still the only one anyone knew anything about, and everything was given to one son.

Four years later, the younger James Chaffin began to have strange dreams. In his sleep, his father would appear at his bedside and just stand in silence. In June 1925 the ghost visited again, this time wearing his black overcoat. For the first time, the ghost spoke. He pulled back his overcoat to show the inside pocket and said that is where his will would be found. Then he vanished.

The next morning James woke up convinced that his father had sent him a message. He went to visit his mother and found the overcoat with the note sealed inside. After reading the note, James got several people together to act as witnesses as he retrieved the *Bible* from his mother's house and found the new will.

Marshall had died by this point, but Marshall's wife and son fought the new will. They took James

James Chaffin was convinced that his father's ghost instructed him to look in his *Bible* to find a hidden copy of his will.

to court. About a week before the trial was to begin the ghost of James Sr. appeared again. His spirit seemed to be restless and kept asking about his old will. The younger James decided this was a sign that he would win the court battle, and he did.

Can a ghost return from the dead to give a message to a loved one? The answer will probably never be known. But for the people mentioned above, their answer is a resounding yes.

Chapter 3

Helpful Ghosts

A visit from a ghost can be a spooky occurrence, but most ghosts do not cause people harm. In fact, some ghosts can be downright helpful.

The Library Ghost

The Topeka and Shawnee County Public Library in Topeka, Kansas, is thought to be home to quite a helpful ghost. Susan Marchant, special collections manager, has experienced several strange happenings at the library. She thinks the events may be caused by a ghost named Mrs. Johnson. Marchant remarked, "I haven't met Mrs. Johnson yet. Or maybe I have; she could be responsible for these other things that happen."[5]

Librarian Susan Marchant believes the doors to her library in Topeka, Kansas, have a haunted history.

Mrs. Johnson was originally said to be a ghost that haunted a house also located in Topeka. That house was full of weird things such as rocking chairs rocking by themselves, footsteps in the hallways, and doors opening and closing by themselves. The house was torn down, but the beautiful front doors now hang at the entry of Marchant's office.

The doors have not opened and closed by themselves but Marchant has witnessed unusual events:

> My desk sits above a security camera [that hangs on the wall] on the next floor down, and I saw one of the security people come up. . . . He said, "The camera [on the next floor down] is panning the hallway." [But] the camera is bolted to the wall and doesn't move. We never did figure out what created that. Maybe Mrs. Johnson wanted a better view of the hallway.[6]

Strange Happenings

Another time, Marchant and a volunteer were searching for a series of books, which just happened to be titled *The Ghosts of Fort Riley*. They could not find the books anywhere, but that was not unusual since the books were small. Suddenly, the volunteer exclaimed that she had seen a stuffed toy lion move.

"He [the lion] had essentially fallen up as opposed to the usual falling down,"[7] Marchant said. When she picked up the lion, he was resting on the books they had been looking for.

No one knows what causes the strange happenings at the library. Marchant says, "It could be Mrs. Johnson just trying to take care of us all, and believe me, we all need to be taken care of."[8]

Finding lost things and putting away items are quite nice things for a ghost to do. Some helpful ghosts, however, go the extra mile. Captain Joshua Slocum was visited by a ghost who may have saved his life.

Captain Slocum's Ghostly Tale

In 1895 Captain Joshua Slocum was sailing his way into the history books as the first man to sail around the world. His trip was not without hardships, however, and he found himself caught in a **squall**. As if that was not bad enough, he was suddenly seized by horrible stomach cramps. He was in such bad shape, he staggered below deck and passed out. His experience is stated here in his own words:

> How long I lay there I could not tell, for I became delirious. When I came to, as I thought, from my swoon, I realized that the sloop was plunging into a heavy sea, and looking out of the companionway, to my amazement I saw a tall man at the helm. His rigid hand, grasping the spokes of the wheel, held them as in a vise. One may imagine my astonishment.

Captain Joshua Slocum believes a ghost helped him to become the first man to sail around the world.

His rig was that of a foreign sailor, and the large red cap he wore was cockbilled over his left ear, and all was set off with shaggy black whiskers. He would have been taken for a pirate in any part of the world. While I gazed upon his threatening aspect I forgot the storm, and wondered if he had come to cut my throat. This he seemed to divine. "Señor," said he, doffing his cap, "I have come to do you no harm." And a smile, the faintest in the world, but still a smile, played on his face, which seemed not unkind when

Helpful Ghosts **25**

he spoke. "I am one of Columbus's crew," he continued. "I am the pilot of the *Pinta* come to aid you. Lie quiet, señor captain," he added, "and I will guide your ship tonight. You have a calentura (stomach cramps), but you will be all right tomorrow. You did wrong, captain, to mix cheese with plums. White cheese is never safe unless you know whence it comes."[9]

Slocum was too weak to do anything but what the ghost suggested, so he slept. The next day he found his ship was still on course. He thought to himself that Christoper Columbus himself could not have done better.

Captain Slocum was lucky that day to have been visited by such a helpful ghost. Some ghosts thrive on protecting people. Perhaps they do not want anyone to die in the same manner in which they did.

Two other protective ghosts are Don Repo and Bob Loft, victims of the crash of Eastern Airlines Flight 401 in the early 1970s.

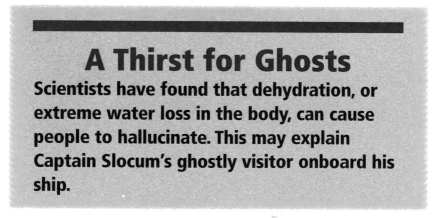

A Thirst for Ghosts

Scientists have found that dehydration, or extreme water loss in the body, can cause people to hallucinate. This may explain Captain Slocum's ghostly visitor onboard his ship.

In this illustration, Joshua Slocum meets the ghost captain of the *Pinta*.

The Ghosts of Flight 401

In December 1972 an Eastern Airlines jet, Flight 401, crashed into a Florida swamp. Among the 101 people who died were the pilot, Bob Loft, and the flight engineer, Don Repo.

After the crash the airline salvaged parts of the destroyed plane. The parts that were not damaged were used to repair other airplanes. These other airplanes received not only salvaged parts but maybe even ghosts.

Pilot Bob Loft (top) and flight engineer Don Repo (bottom) were killed in the crash of Flight 40 (below). Their ghosts have been seen on several Eastern Airlines flights.

Ghost-Hunting Tools

Ghost hunting is a high-tech endeavor. Tools such as normal and infrared cameras, tape recorders, electromagnetic detectors, and thermal imagers help ghost hunters eliminate factual explanations for ghostly events. Events that cannot be explained might be proof of a ghost.

A ghost hunter uses a sophisticated device to search for evidence of ghostly activity at a monastery in Rhode Island.

Encounters with the ghosts of Loft and Repo have been reported on more than twenty occasions. The **apparitions** have been seen by other pilots, flight attendants, mechanics, and passengers.

It appears that the ghosts of Loft and Repo are devoted to protecting the passengers and crew of the airplanes that carry parts of Flight 401. This mission was evident when the spirit of Repo visited one airline captain. Repo told him, "There will never be another crash. We will not let it happen." And just before a plane was to take off, Repo reported to a flight engineer, "You don't need to worry about the pre-flight [inspection]. I've already done it."[10]

A Curious Encounter

A flight attendant named Faye Merryweather also had a curious encounter with Repo. His face appeared to be looking at her from inside an oven in the airplane's kitchen. She immediately called two coworkers, who instantly recognized Repo. He warned the crew to watch out for fire on the plane. The crew learned to take Repo's warnings seriously, as later in the flight the plane experienced engine trouble and had to cancel the last portion of its flight.

Encountering a ghost would certainly be scary. If one must meet a ghost, however, a helpful ghost would certainly be one of the better spirits to have around.

For the most part, ghosts are harmless. They may be mischievous, and some enjoy playing pranks on the living, but generally they do not have any desire to harm anyone. There are always exceptions to the rule, however. Tales of encounters with dangerous ghosts do exist.

The Suicidal Ghost

One such encounter took place in 1806. A group of soldiers was stationed near a house in Dorset County in England, guarding against an attack from France. The general was invited to dine at the nearby house. The general accepted and brought along one of his younger staff members.

This photograph showing a woman kneeling in prayer before a ghostly figure was proved to be a fake.

During dinner the general noticed that the young soldier was behaving very rudely. He was openly staring at the hostess of the dinner party with a look of horror on his face.

Suddenly, the young soldier jumped up and ran from the room. The general rushed after the young man, thinking he had gone insane. As the general ran outside, he saw that the young soldier had jumped on his horse and ridden away.

The general immediately gave chase and caught up with the young man. He asked the young man what in the world was going on. The young man replied that he had seen a hooded figure standing close behind the hostess of the party. The ghostly image was trying to convince the woman to commit suicide.

The general scoffed at this explanation, thinking the soldier had truly gone crazy. Just then, one of the servants from the house galloped up on another horse. The general called to him to ask what he was doing. The servant replied he was going to fetch the doctor, but he feared it was too late. The servant then reported that just after the men left, the woman picked up a table knife and cut her throat right in front of everyone.

Ghosts on Film

Photographs of ghosts are not uncommon, but most turn out to be fakes. William Mumler took one such photo in 1865. He claimed it showed the ghost of Abraham Lincoln standing behind his widow Mary. Mumler was exposed as a fraud after people recognized the "ghosts" in this and other Mumler photos as living people posing as ghosts.

Why in the world this hooded figure goaded the poor woman into committing suicide is not known. Though the ghost itself did not harm the woman, it certainly was a dangerous presence. There are also tales of ghosts that physically strike people, such as the story of James Durham.

A Ghost and His Dog

James Durham worked as a night watchman at a railroad station in Darlington, England. Everyone who knew Durham, knew he was a hard worker and an honest man. One night on the job, Durham had an eerie experience.

As the night was a cold one, Durham went inside to warm himself by the small fire that was kept burning. Almost the moment he sat down, he noticed a strange man enter the room. The man was followed by a big black dog. As Durham watched

The Society for Psychical Research

Formed in London in 1882, the Society for Psychical Research was the first official organization dedicated to investigating ghosts. By the year 1900, the society had compiled 11,000 pages of ghost reports.

the man, the man stared right back with a kind of curious smile on his face.

The man was dressed in a rather old-fashioned manner, with a high stand-up collar, a cutaway coat with gold buttons, and a cap. All at once Durham saw the man strike out with his arm, and he had the feeling of being hit. Durham jumped up with his own fists ready. He threw a punch back at the man, but his fist seemed to go right through him, striking the fireplace on the other side and skinning Durham's knuckles.

Not all ghosts are human. Some people have reported encounters with the ghosts of animals like this rottweiler.

The punch seemed to connect with the man, however, sending him back toward the fire with a strange and unearthly sound. Instantly, the dog sprang upon Durham and seemed to grip him on the calf of his leg.

When the man recovered, he called off his dog with a click of his tongue and disappeared into another room. Durham immediately followed the man and dog, but when he looked into the room, there was no one there. There was no way for the man to have escaped the building except to have used the door that was behind Durham.

Durham described this event in a letter to England's Society for Psychical Research. He ended his letter by saying he was certain that what he had seen was ghostly.

Perhaps the ghost Durham encountered just wanted him to leave what the ghost considered his space. Some dangerous ghosts return for entirely different reasons, though, such as revenge.

Ghostly Revenge

In the summer of 1884 four men survived the shipwreck of the British yacht *Pierrot*. Three of the men—Edward Rutt, Josh Dudley, and Will Hoon—were rescued after floating in the ocean in a small lifeboat for nearly a month. The fourth, Dick Tomlin, was dead by the time the rescuers arrived. It would not have been unthinkable that Tomlin had died from starvation or **exposure**, but to the rescuers' horror his body appeared partially eaten.

Rutt, Dudley, and Hoon finally admitted that they had eaten their shipmate to avoid starvation after he had died of natural causes. Upon inspection of the body, a new cause of death was found. The sailors had apparently stabbed their shipmate and then consumed his body.

When the men were returned to England, they were tried and convicted of murder and sentenced to a mere six months in prison. When their jail time was up, Josh Dudley found a job driving a large freight wagon. Two weeks after he started his new job, the horses he was driving were scared by something in the middle of the street. The horses ran wildly, throwing Dudley from the wagon. He hit his head on the cobblestone street and died.

The three survivors of the shipwrecked *Pierrot* later met with mysterious deaths that some blamed on the ghost of a shipmate they murdered.

A Million Dollar Ghost

Magician and ghost skeptic James Randi has offered $1 million to anyone who can prove the existence of ghosts. So far, his money is safe.

Magician James Randi is one of the world's most famous ghost skeptics.

Witnesses of the accident reported seeing a strange figure standing in the street, just before the horses bolted. They said it looked like a man wrapped from head to toe in bloodstained bandages. Right after the accident, however, the figure vanished.

Rutt heard about the death of his friend and became frightened. He was sure a relative of Tomlin was after him. He sought out Hoon to warn him, but

Hoon had become a hopeless drunk. His excessive drinking had made him so sick, he was taken to a hospital. Shortly after his arrival, he died in a violent fit.

The people who witnessed Hoon's death at the hospital reported that another patient, covered in bloody bandages, was holding Hoon down as he screamed and thrashed about in his bed. No one was sure who the mysterious patient had been.

When Rutt heard of this incident he was scared stiff. He did not know if it was Tomlin's ghost or someone else, but Rutt was sure someone or something was out to get him.

Rutt went to the police for help, but they just laughed at him. He was so desperate, however, the police offered to lock him in a jail cell for protection. Rutt gladly accepted.

Around 3 A.M., guards heard screams coming from Rutt's cell. They hurried to the cell and unlocked it, but they were too late. Rutt lay dead in a corner of the cell. Clutched in his hands were a few shreds of bandages, covered in blood.

Do Ghosts Exist?

So are there such things as ghosts? Maybe there are or maybe there are not. Many have the same opinion as the **Marquise Du Deffand** of France. When asked if she believed in ghosts she replied, "Oh, no, but I am afraid of them."[11]

Whether they are figments of the imagination or supernatural wonders, ghosts will continue to fascinate people the world over.

Notes

Chapter 1: The World of Ghosts

1. Quoted in Paranormal Phenomena on About.com, "Ghosts: What Are They?" http://paranormal.about.com/library/weekly/aa082701a.htm.
2. Quoted in Prince Michael of Greece, *Living with Ghosts, Eleven Extraordinary Tales*. London: W.W. Norton, 1995, pp. 9–10.

Chapter 2: Messenger Ghosts

3. Quoted in Hilary Evans and Patrick Huyghe, *The Field Guide to Ghosts and Other Apparitions*. New York: Quill, 2000, p 94.
4. Quoted in Patricia Telesco, *Ghosts, Spirits, and Hauntings*. Freedom, CA: Crossing, 1999, pp. 36–37.

Chapter 3: Helpful Ghosts

5. Quoted in Brandy Nance, "At Library, Ghosts Tend to Be Tidy," *Topeka Capital Journal*, October 31, 2004. www.cjonline.com/stories/103104/index.shtml.
6. Quoted in Nance, "At Library, Ghosts Tend to Be Tidy."

7. Quoted in Nance, "At Library, Ghosts Tend to Be Tidy."

8. Quoted in Nance, "At Library, Ghosts Tend to Be Tidy."

9. Joshua Slocum, *Sailing Alone Around the World,* 1900. Reprint, Mineola, NY: Dover, 1956, pp. 41–45.

10. Quoted in Near-Death Experiences and the Afterlife, "The Ghosts of Flight 401, John G. Fuller's Paranormal Research." www.near dcath.com/ghosts.html.

Chapter 4: Dangerous Ghosts

11. Quoted in Harry Marks, "Top Ten Haunted Locations," Winter Steel.com. www.winter steel.com/Top_Ten_Haunted_Locations.html.

Glossary

apparitions: Visual appearances of ghosts.

exposure: Being subjected to extreme weather.

Grecian: Being from the country of Greece.

hieroglyphics: A system of writing that uses pictures for words.

historian: One who studies and records history.

manacles: A device that restrains the hands like handcuffs.

Marquise Du Deffand: French society woman who lived from 1697–1780, famous for her "salons" or gatherings for conversation and readings.

philosopher: Someone who pursues wisdom through logic.

squall: A brief but violent windstorm, usually with rain or snow.

supernatural: Relating to existence outside of the natural world.

For Further Exploration

Books

Jacqueline Laks Gorman, *Ghosts*. Milwaukee, WI: Gareth Stevens, 2002. Find out about ghost ships and trains, spiritualism, the haunted White House, and other stories in this exciting book.

Joan Holub, *The Haunted States of America*. New York: Aladdin, 2001. An entertaining series of ghost stories from all 50 states and Canada.

Michael Martin, *Ghosts*. Mankato, MN: Capstone, 2005. This book gives a great overview of ghosts and features some interesting ghost stories.

Jason Rich, *The Everything Ghost Book*. Avon, MA: Adams, 2001. From spooky stories to unexplained mysteries, this information-packed book is a fantastic source of ghost information.

Graham Watkins, *Ghosts and Poltergeists*. New York: Rosen, 2002. Fascinating case studies of ghost encounters fill this book. Also included are theories for ghost sightings.

Web Sites

Gettysburg Ghosts (www.gettysburgghosts.net/ ghost_hunting.htm). A site dedicated to the paranormal, with ghost pictures, ghost sounds, and information on ghost-hunting equipment.

Ghosts of the Prairie (www.prairieghosts.com). A truly ghostly site that explores haunted places across the United States. It is packed with information like haunted history articles, ghost-hunting articles, and the haunted highways of America.

National Ghost Hunters Society Kids Page (www.nationalghosthunters.com/kids.html). Full of games, pictures, and stories about ghosts.

Index

Picture Credits

About the Author

Kelli M. Brucken is the author of many works of nonfiction for children. Other books she has written for KidHaven Press include *Bristlecone Pines* and *Banshees*. She makes her home in Auburn, Kansas, with her husband and two children.